oasis

SONY MUSIC PUBLISHING

GO LET IT OUT

1. PAINT NO ILLUSION, TRY TO CLICK WITH WHATCHA GOT
   TASTE EVERY POTION COS IF YER LIKE YERSELF A LOT
   GO LET IT OUT, GO LET IT IN, GO LET IT OUT

2. LIFE IS PRECOCIOUS IN A MOST PECULIAR WAY
   SISTER PSYCHOSIS DON'T GOT A LOT TO SAY
   SHE GO LET IT OUT, SHE GO LET IT IN, SHE GO LET IT OUT
   SHE GO LET IT OUT, SHE GO LET IT IN, SHE GO LET IT OUT

   IS IT ANY WONDER WHY PRINCES & KINGS
   ARE CLOWNS THAT CAPER IN THEIR SAWDUST RINGS
   AND ORDINARY PEOPLE THAT ARE LIKE YOU AND ME
   WE'RE THE KEEPERS OF THEIR DESTINY

3. I'M GOIN LEAVING THIS CITY,I'M GOIN DRIVIN' OUTTA TOWN
   YOUR COMIN' WITH ME THE RIGHT TIME IS ALWAYS NOW
   TO GO LET IT OUT, GO LET IT IN, GO LET IT OUT
   TO GO LET IT OUT, GO LET IT IN, GO LET IT OUT

   IS IT ANY WONDER WHY PRINCES AND KINGS
   ARE CLOWNS THAT CAPER IN THEIR SAWDUST RINGS
   COS ORDINARY PEOPLE THAT ARE LIKE YOU AND ME
   WE'RE THE BUILDERS OF THEIR DESTINY

   SO GO LET IT OUT - GO LET IT IN
   GO LET IT OUT - DON'T LET IT IN
   GO LET IT OUT - GO LET IT IN
   GO LET IT OUT - DON'T LET IT - DON'T LET IT IN

WHO FEELS LOVE?

1. FOUND WHAT I'D LOST INSIDE
   MY SPIRIT HAS BEEN PURIFIED
   TAKE A THORN FROM MY PRIDE
   AND HAND IN HAND WE'LL TAKE A WALK OUTSIDE

   THANK YOU FOR THE SUN THE ONE THAT SHINES ON EVERYONE
   WHO FEELS LOVE
   NOW THERE'S A MILLION YEARS BETWEEN MY FANTASIES & FEARS
   I FEEL LOVE

2. I'M LEAVING ALL THAT I SEE
   NOW ALL MY EMOTIONS FILL THE AIR I BREATH

   NOW YOU UNDERSTAND THAT THIS IS NOT THE PROMISED LAND
   THEY SPOKE OF
   THERE'S NOTHING MORE TO BE
   IF YOU CAN BE THE REMEDY WHO HEALS LOVE

PUT YER MONEY WHERE YER MOUTH IS

1. PUT YER MONEY WHERE YER MOUTH IS
   YER MAMMA SEZ THAT YOU WAS REAL
   PUT YER MONEY WHERE YER MOUTH IS
   YER MAMMA SEZ THAT YOU WAS REAL

   READY OR NOT, COME WHAT MAY
   THE BETS ARE GOING DOWN FOR JUDGEMENT DAY
   SO PUT YER MONEY IN YER MOUTH
   AND YOUR HANDS RIGHT UPON THE WHEEL

2. PUT YER MONEY WHERE YER MOUTH IS
   YER PAPPA SEZ THAT YOU WAS REAL
   PUT YER MONEY WHERE YER MOUTH IS
   YER PAPPA SEZ THAT YOU WAS REAL

   READY OR NOT, AND COME WHAT MAY
   YOU BETCHA GOING DOWN ON JUDGEMENT DAY
   SO PUT YER MONEY IN YER MOUTH
   AND YER HANDS RIGHT UPON THE WHEEL

LITTLE JAMES

1. LITTLE JAMES, WE'RE ALL THE SAME
   THEY ALWAYS SEEM TO LOOK TO US
   BUT WE WEREN'T MEANT TO BE GROWN UPS
   THANK YOU FOR YOUR SMILE
   YOU MAKE IT ALL WORTHWHILE TO US

2. YOU LIVE FOR YOUR TOYS, EVEN THOUGH THEY MAKE NOISE
   HAVE YOU EVER PLAYED WITH PLASTERCINE
   OR EVEN TRIED A TRAMPOLINE
   THANK YOU FOR YOUR SMILE
   YOU MAKE IT ALL WORTHWHILE TO US

   I'M SINGING THIS SONG FOR YOU AND YOUR MUM THAT'S ALL
   'COS IT WON'T BE LONG BEFORE EVERYONE IS GONE

3. SAILED OUT TO SEA, YOUR MUM YOU AND ME
   YOU SWAM THE OCEAN LIKE A CHILD
   LIFE AROUND US WAS SO WILD
   THANK YOU FOR YOUR SMILE
   YOU MAKE IT ALL WORTHWHILE TO US

   I'M SINGING THIS SONG FOR YOU AND YOUR MUM THAT'S ALL
   AND IT WON'T BE LONG BEFORE EVERYONE IS GONE.

GAS PANIC!

1. WHAT TONGUELESS GHOST OF SIN CREPT THROUGH MY CURTAINS?
   SAILING ON A SEA OF SWEAT ON A STORMY NIGHT
   I THINK HE DON'T GOT A NAME BUT I CAN'T BE CERTAIN
   AND IN ME HE STARTS TO CONFIDE

   THAT MY FAMILY DON'T SEEM SO FAMILIAR
   AND MY ENEMIES ALL KNOW MY NAME
   AND IF YOU HEAR ME TAP ON YOUR WINDOW
   BETTER GET ON YER KNEES AND PRAY PANIC IS ON THE WAY

2. MY PULSE PUMPS OUT A BEAT TO THE GHOST DANCER
   MY EYES ARE DEAD AND MY THROAT'S LIKE A BLACK HOLE
   AND IF THERE'S A GOD WOULD HE GIVE ANOTHER CHANCER
   AN HOUR TO SING FOR HIS SOUL

   COS MY FAMILY DON'T SEEM SO FAMILIAR
   AND MY ENEMIES ALL KNOW MY NAME
   AND WHEN YOU HEAR ME TAP ON YER WINDOW
   YER BETTER GET ON YER KNEES AND PRAY PANIC IS ON THE WAY

   COS MY FAMILY DON'T SEEM SO FAMILIAR
   AND MY ENEMIES ALL KNOW MY NAME
   AND WHEN YOU HEAR ME TAP ON YER WINDOW
   THEN YOU GET ON YOUR KNEES AND YOU BETTER PRAY
   COS MY FAMILY DON'T SEEM SO FAMILIAR
   AND MY ENEMIES ALL KNOW MY NAME
   AND WHEN YOU HEAR ME TAP ON YOUR WINDOW
   YER BETTER GET ON YER KNEES AND PRAY
   PANIC IS ON THE WAY
   PANIC IS ON THE WAY

WHERE DID IT ALL GO WRONG?

1. YOU KNOW THAT FEELING YOU GET
   YOU FEEL YOU'RE OLDER THAN TIME
   YOU AIN'T EXACTLY SURE
   IF YOU'VE BEEN AWAY A WHILE

2. DO YOU KEEP THE RECEIPTS
   FOR THE FRIENDS THAT YOU BUY
   AND AIN'T IT BITTERSWEET
   YOU WERE ONLY JUST GETTING BY

   BUT I HOPE YOU KNOW
   THAT IT WON'T LET GO
   IT STICKS AROUND WITH YOU UNTIL THE DAY YOU DIE
   AND I HOPE YOU KNOW THAT IT'S TOUCH AND GO
   I HOPE THE TEARS DON'T STAIN THE WORLD THAT WAITS OUTSIDE
   WHERE DID IT ALL GO WRONG?

3. AND UNTIL YOU'VE REPAID
   THE DREAMS YOU BOUGHT FOR YOUR LIES
   YOU'LL BE CAST AWAY
   ALONE UNDER THE STORMY SKIES

   BUT I HOPE YOU KNOW
   THAT IT WON'T LET GO
   IT STICKS AROUND WITH YOU UNTIL THE DAY YOU DIE
   AND I HOPE YOU KNOW THAT IT'S TOUCH AND GO
   I HOPE THE TEARS DON'T STAIN THE WORLD THAT WAITS OUTSIDE
   WHERE DID IT ALL GO WRONG?

SUNDAY MORNING CALL

1. HERE'S ANOTHER SUNDAY MORNING CALL
   YER HEAR YER HEAD-A-BANGING ON THE DOOR
   SLIP YOUR SHOES ON AND THEN OUT YOU CRAWL
   INTO A DAY THAT COULDN'T GIVE YOU MORE
   BUT WHAT FOR?

   AND IN YOUR HEAD DO YOU FEEL
   WHAT YOU'RE NOT SUPPOSED TO FEEL
   YOU TAKE WHAT YOU WANT
   BUT YOU WON'T GET IT FOR FREE
   YOU NEED MORE TIME
   COS YOUR THOUGHTS AND WORDS WON'T LAST FOREVER MORE
   BUT I'M NOT SURE IF IT EVER WORKS OUT RIGHT
   BUT IT'S OK. IT'S ALL RIGHT

2. WHEN YER LONELY AND YOU START TO HEAR
   THE LITTLE VOICES IN YOUR HEAD AT NIGHT
   YOU WILL ONLY SNIFF AWAY THE TEARS
   SO YOU CAN DANCE UNTIL THE MORNING LIGHT
   AT WHAT PRICE

   AND IN YOUR HEAD DO YOU FEEL
   WHAT YOU'RE NOT SUPPOSED TO FEEL
   YOU TAKE WHAT YOU WANT
   BUT YOU WON'T GET IT FOR FREE
   YOU NEED MORE TIME
   COS YOUR THOUGHTS AND WORDS WON'T LAST FOREVER MORE
   BUT I'M NOT SURE IF IT EVER WORKS OUT RIGHT
   BUT IT'S OK. IT'S ALL RIGHT

   AND IN YOUR HEAD DO YOU FEEL
   WHAT YOU'RE NOT SUPPOSED TO FEEL
   WHEN YOU TAKE WHAT YOU WANT
   YOU DON'T GET HOPE FOR FREE
   YOU NEED MORE TIME
   COS YOUR THOUGHTS AND WORDS WON'T LAST FOREVER MORE
   AND I'M NOT SURE IF IT'LL EVER, EVER, EVER WORK OUT RIGHT
   WILL IT EVER, EVER, EVER WORK OUT RIGHT?
   COS IT NEVER, NEVER, NEVER WORKS OUT RIGHT

I CAN SEE A LIAR

1. BABY THE TIME IS RIGHT TO TELL IT ALL LIKE IT IS
   AND NOW THAT I FEEL GOD LIKE THERE'S NOTHING THAT CAN'T BE KISSED
   THE NAME OF A LONELY SOUL IS SCRATCHED INTO MY BRAIN
   HE THOUGHT HE WAS KING CREOLE
   UNTIL HE FOUND OUT, UNTIL HE FOUND OUT

   HE SITS UPON A THRONE
   HE LIVES A SLEAZY LIE
   BUT HE'S ALL ALONE AGAIN, AGAIN

   I CAN SEE A LIAR, SITTING BY THE FIRE
   TROUBLE IN HIS HEART, LAUGHING AT THE THOUGHT
   COMING AS HE GOES INTO OVERDOSE
   I WONDER WHAT HE THINKS OF ME?

ROLL IT OVER

1. I CAN GIVE A HUNDRED MILLION REASONS
   TO BUILD A BARRICADE
   I BLAME IT ON THE CHANGING OF THE SEASONS
   THE THOUGHTS THAT I'VE CONVEYED

   DOES IT MAKE IT ALL RIGHT?
   IT DOESN'T MAKE IT ALL RIGHT

   TO ROLL IT OVER MY SOUL AND LEAVE ME HERE
   ROLL IT OVER MY SOUL AND LEAVE ME HERE

2. LOOK AROUND AT ALL THE PLASTIC PEOPLE
   WHO LIVE WITHOUT A CARE
   TRY TO SIT WITH ME AROUND MY TABLE
   BUT NEVER BRING A CHAIR

FUCKIN' IN THE BUSHES

Words & Music by Noel Gallagher

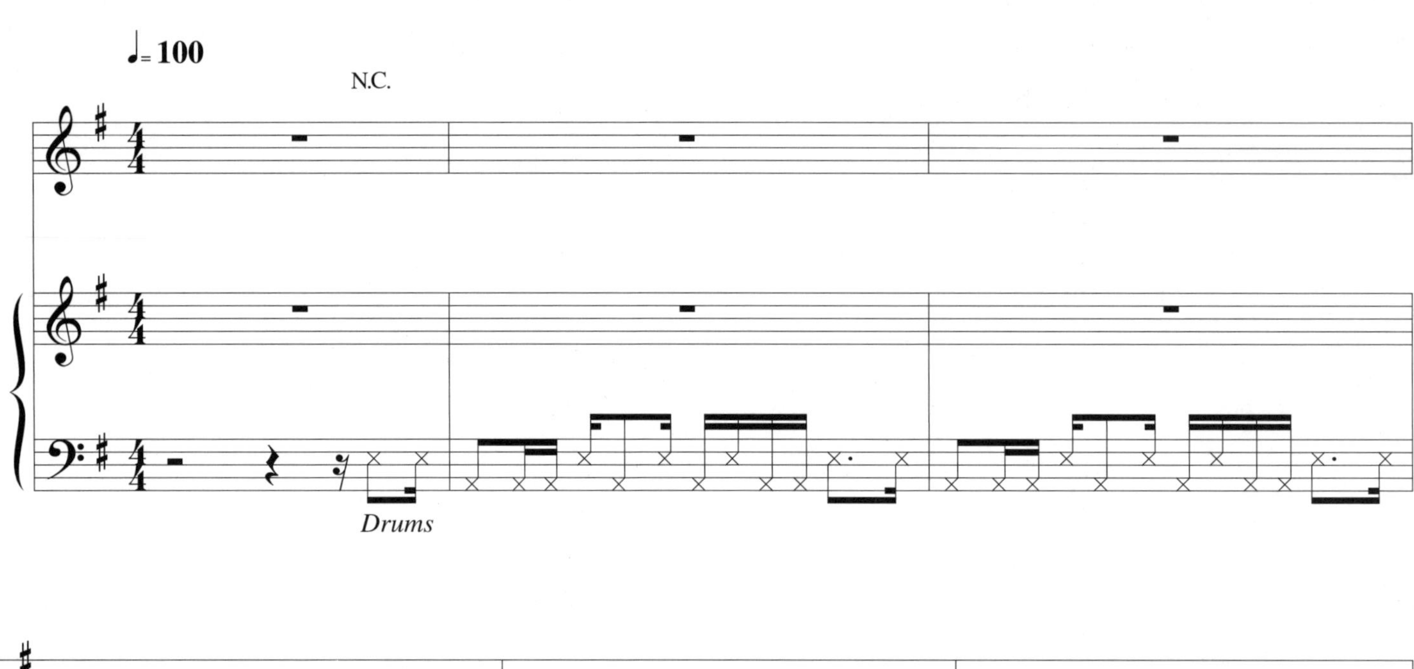

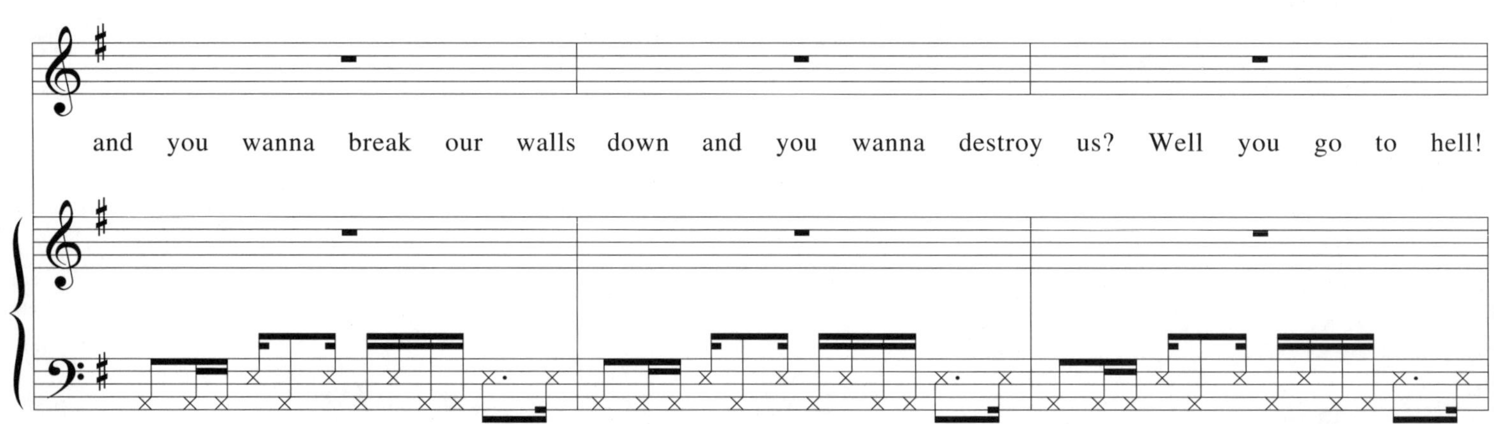

Em
Drums cont. sim.

G
F#m7
Fmaj7
Em
G
F#m7
Fmaj7
Em
To Coda G
F#m7
Fmaj7
Em

G
F#m7
Fmaj7
Em
Am
Cmaj7/G
F#m7(b5)
Fmaj7

Em
Cmaj7/G
F#m7(b5)
Fmaj7
D.%. al Coda
Coda
Am
Cmaj7/G
(1º Spoken) Kids running around naked, fucking in the bushes,

F#m7(b5)
Fmaj7
kids running around naked, fucking in the bushes,
Am
Cmaj7/G
kids running around naked, fucking in the bushes,
F#m7(b5)
1.
Fmaj7
2.
Fmaj7
kids running around naked, fucking in the bushes.
Em
Repeat to fade

GO LET IT OUT

Words & Music by Noel Gallagher

D/A

like your-self a lot, go let it out, go let it in,

F add 9   G   A7

and go let it out. Spoken: (Pick up the bass)

A7

2. Life is pre-co-cious in the most pe-cu-liar way,
(Verse 3 see block lyric)

sis-ter psy-cho-sis, don't got a lot to say. She go let it out,

D
Fadd9
G
she go let it in, she go let it out.
A
D
She go let it out, she go let it in,
Fadd9
G
A7
she go let it out.
D
F
A
C%
D
F
Is it a-ny won-der why prin - ces and kings are clowns that ca-per in their

A   C6/9   D   F#   A   C6/9
saw-dust rings?_ Or-di-na-ry peo-ple that are like you and me,__ we're the
G7   D5   G7
keep-ers of their des - ti - ny.___ We're the keep-ers of their des - ti - ny.__
(2° build-ers)   (build-ers)
1.
D5   A7
(Ooh!)   3. I'm gon-na
2.
D5   G7
We're the build-ers of their des - ti - ny.__

D5
G7
D
Dsus4
We're the build-ers of their des - ti - ny.
D5add#11
Dsus4
D
Dsus4
D5add#11
Dsus4
D
Dsus4
D5add#11
Dsus4
D
Dsus4
D5add#11
So go let it out,

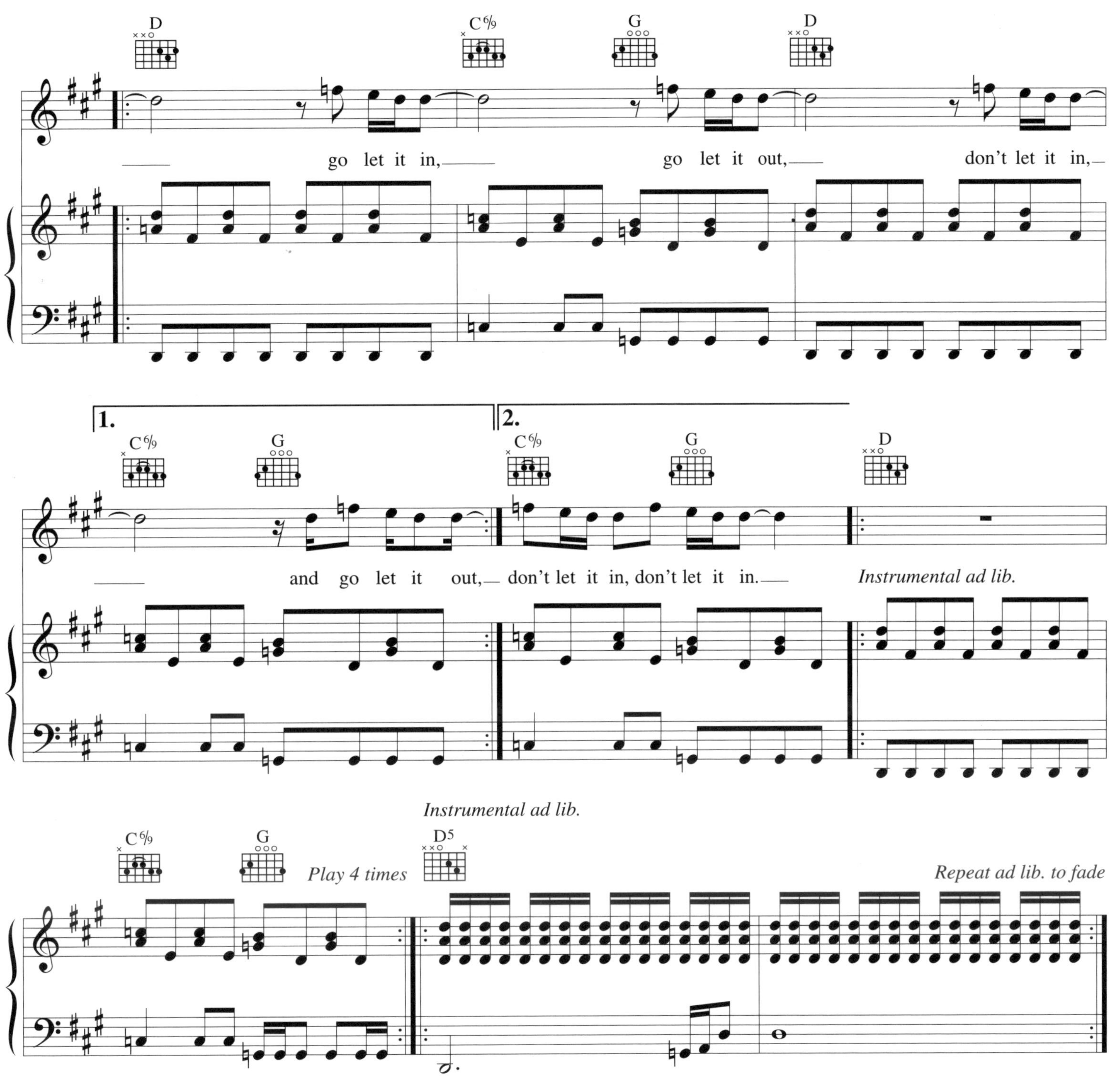

Verse 3:
I'm goin' leavin' the city
I'm goin' drivin' outta town
And you're comin' with me
The right time is always now.

So go let it out
And go let it in
And go let it out.
So go let it out
So go let it in
And go let it out.

Is it any wonder *etc.*

WHO FEELS LOVE?

Words & Music by Noel Gallagher

been pu - ri - fied.

Take a thorn from my pride and hand
(Verse 2 see block lyric)

in hand we'll take a walk out - side.

Thank-you for the sun, the one that shines on ev-'ry-one who feels love.

G5

Bb6/9

Am7

Cadd9

G/B
Bb6/9
Am7
Now there's a mil-lion years be-tween my fan-ta-sies and fears. I feel
G5
love.
1.
2. I'm
2. G
G/F
Em7
G/D
G
G/F
Em7
G/D

G
G/F
Em7
G/D
G
G/F
Em7
E♭maj7aug
fr3
G5
Guitar
B♭6/9
Am7
G5

Bb6/9
Am7
Cadd9
G/B
Bb6/9
Am7
Cadd9
G/B
Bb6/9
Am7
Cadd9
I thank
you for the sun, the one that shines on ev-'ry-one who feels love.
24

Verse 2:
I'm leaving all that I see
Now all my emotions
Fill the air I breathe.

Now you understand that
This is not the promised land they spoke of
There's nothing more to be
If you can be the remedy who heals love.

PUT YER MONEY WHERE YER MOUTH IS

Words & Music by Noel Gallagher

Tune guitar down a semitone

Put yer mo - ney where yer mouth is yer ma - ma sez that you was re -
- al. Rea - dy or not and
come what may, the bets are go - in' down for judge - ment day. So put yer
mo-ney in yer mouth and yer hands right up - on the wheel.

E♭5
(E5)
G♭5
(G5)
A♭5
(A5)
G♭5
(G5)
E♭5
(E5)
G♭5
(G5)
A♭5
(A5)
G♭5
(G5)
fr3
fr5
fr3
fr3
fr5
fr3
2. Put yer
2, 3.
G♭5
(G5)
E♭m
(Em)
/D♭
(/D)
fr3
(Ah
E♭m
(Em)
/G♭
(/G)
E♭m
(Em)
/D♭
(/D)
—)
(Ah
A♭9
(A9)
fr6
To Coda ⊕
D.C. al Coda
)

Verse 2:
Put yer money where yer mouth is
Yer papa sez that you was real
Put yer money where yer mouth is
Yer papa sez that you was real
Ready or not and come what may
You betcha goin' down on judgement day
So put yer money in yer mouth
And yer hands right upon the wheel.

Verse 3:
Put yer money where yer mouth is
Yer mama sez that you was real
Put yer money where yer mouth is
Yer mama sez that you was real
Ready or not and come what may
The bets are goin' down for judgement day
So put yer money in yer mouth
And yer hands right upon the wheel.

LITTLE JAMES

Words & Music by Liam Gallagher

G
make it all worth - while to us.
G
2. Live for your toys, even though they make noise. Have you
(Verse 3 see block lyric)
F6
ev - er played with plas - ti - cine, ev - en tried a tram - po - line?
C
Thank - you for your smile, you make it all worth - while to us.

G
F6
I'm sing - ing this song____ for
C
G
you and your mom____ and that's all.____
F6
C
G
It won't be long____ be - fore ev - 'ry - one____ is gone.____
F6

Verse 3:
Sailed out to sea
Your mum, you and me
You swam the oceans like a child
Life around us was so wild
Thankyou for your smile
You make it all worthwhile to us.

I'm singing this song *etc.*

GAS PANIC!

Words & Music by Noel Gallagher

Bbm/Db
(Am/C)
Ab6/9
(G6/9)
Bb5
(A5)
- ing on a sea of sweat on a storm-y night. I
Bbm/Db
(Am/C)
Ab6/9
(G6/9)
Bb5
(A5)
think he don t got a name but I can t be cer - tain and in
Bbm/Db
(Am/C)
Ab6/9
(G6/9)
Bb5
(A5)
me he starts to con - fide. That my fam -
Bbm/Db
(Am/C)
Ab6/9
(G6/9)
Bb5
(A5)
Bbm/Db
(Am/C)
Ab6/9
(G6/9)
- ily don t seem so fa - mi - liar, and my en - em - ies all know my name.

And if you hear me tap on your win-dow
(when)
you'd bet-ter
get on your knees and pray, pan-ic is on the way.
1.
2.
2. My
36

A♭ add 9
(G add 9)
fr3
E♭
(D)
B♭
(A)
A♭ add 9
(G add 9)
fr3
E♭
(D)
D♭6
(C6)
E♭
(D)
D♭6
(C6)
E♭
(D)
B♭5
(A5)
D♭6
(C6)
E♭
(D)

Bb5 (A5)
Db6 (C6)
Eb (D)
Bb5 (A5)
Eb (D)
Fsus4 (Esus4)
F (E)
Coz my fam-
Db6 (C6)
Eb (D)
Bb5 (A5)
Db6 (C6)
Eb (D)
-ily don't seem so fa-mi-liar, and my en-em-ies all know my name.
Bb5 (A5)
Db6 (C6)
Eb (D)
Bb5 (A5)
1.
And when you hear me tap on your win-dow then you get-

2.
Db6 (C6)
Eb (D)
Bb5 (A5)
Bb5 (A5)
on your knees and you bet-ter pray. Coz my fam - dow. You'd bet-ter
Eb (D)
Fsus4 (Esus4)
get on your knees and pray, pan-ic is on the way.
Db6 (C6)
Eb (D)
Bb (A)
Db6 (C6)
Eb (D)
Bb (A)
Db6 (C6)
Eb (D)
Bb (A)
Pan-ic is on the way.

Verse 2:
My pulse pumps out a beat to the ghost dancer
My eyes are dead and my throat s like a black hole
And if there s a God, would he give another chancer
An hour to sing for his soul.

Coz my family don t seem so familiar *etc.*

SUNDAY MORNING CALL

Words & Music by Noel Gallagher

Dm
D
But what for? And in your head
G
D
Em7
do you feel what you're not sup - posed to feel?
C
G
D
And you take what you want, but you don't
(won't
F
Em
D
G
) get it for free. You need more time
(hope)
42

D   Em7   C
coz your thoughts____ and words__ won't last________ for - ev - er - more.__

To Coda

G   D   Em
____ And I'm not sure________ if it - 'll ev - - er work__ out right.

C   D5   D5/C   G/B   C5add9
____ But it's O. K.________ It's al - right.

Con pedale

1.
D5   D5/C   G/B

2.
G/B   Bb
Guitar

Gm
F
Gm
Bb
C
Bb
C
Bb/F
Gm
F
Gm
Bb
C
Bb
C
D
C
D
D.%. al Coda
And   in   your   head

Verse 2:
When you're lonely and you start to hear
The little voices in your head at night
You will only sniff away the tears
So you can dance until the morning light
At what price?

And in your head *etc.*

WHERE DID IT ALL GO WRONG?

Words & Music by Noel Gallagher

Cmaj7
D sus 4/2
fr5
Em7
You ain't ex - act - ly sure if you've been a - way a while.
D
Em7
D
2. Do you keep the re - ceipts
Em7
D
Cmaj7
for the friends that you buy? And ain't it bit - ter - sweet,
D sus 4/2
fr5
A7sus4
C6/9
you were on - ly just get - ting by. But I

Em
Em7
Dsus4/2 fr5
hope you know___ that it won't let go.   It sticks a - round_ with you un - til   the day_ you die.
Asus4
Em
Em7
___   And I   hope you know___   that it's   touch and go,   I hope the tears
Dsus4/2 fr5
Asus4
To Coda
___ don't stain the world_ that   waits_ out - side.___   Where_ did it all go___
Cmaj9
Em7
D
___ wrong?
48

Em7
D
Em7
3. And un - til you've re - paid
D
Em7
D
the dreams you bought for your lies
Cmaj7
Dsus4/2
fr5
A7sus4
you'll be cast a - way, a - lone un - der storm-y skies,
C6/9
A7sus4
C6/9
D.%. al Coda
a - lone un - der storm-y skies. But I

Coda
Cadd9
Guitar
G
D
Em7
wrong?
Cadd9
G
D
Em7
Cadd9
G
D
Em7
Cadd9
B7
8vb
But I
Em7
Em9
hope you know that it won't let go. It sticks a - round

D sus 4/2
Asus4
Em7
with you un-til the day_ you die._ And I hope you know_ that it's
Em9
D sus 4/2
touch and go, I hope the tears_ don't stain the world_ that waits_ out-side.
1.
Asus4
And I
2.
Asus4
Where_ did it all go_
Cmaj9
wrong?
G
Em

I CAN SEE A LIAR

Words & Music by Noel Gallagher

D5   D5/C#   D5/C   G/B
1. Ba - by the time is right to tell it all like it is.

D5   D5/C#
And now that I feel god - like there's

D5/C   G/B
no - thing that can't be kissed.

D5   D5/C#   D5/C   G/B
2. The name of a lone - ly soul is scratched in - to my brain.
(Verse 3 see block lyric)

D5
D5/C♯
He thought he was King Creole un-
D5/C
G/B
B♭
-til he found out, 'til he found out.
He sits up-
C5
D5
-on a throne, he lives a slea-zy lie,
B♭
Asus4
Csus2
but he's all a-lone a-gain, a-gain.

D5 Csus2 D5 [G]
I can see a li - ar sit - ting by the fire.

D5 Csus2 D5 [G]
Trou - ble in his heart. Laugh-

D5 Csus2 D5 [G]
-ing at the thought com - ing as he goes, in - to ov - er - dose. I

G5 1. 2.
won - der what he thinks of me.

Bb
F
G5
Bb
F
Asus4
Csus2
D5
Csus2
D5
[G]
D5
Csus2
D5
[G]
Ba - by you're a li - ar
sit - ting by the fire.
D5
Csus2
D5
[G]
Trou - ble in your heart.
You're laugh-

Verse 3:
Maybe the time is right
To tell it all like it is
And now that I feel godlike
There's nothing that can't be kissed
He sits upon a throne
He lives a sleazy lie
But he's all alone again, again.

I can see a liar *etc.*

ROLL IT OVER

Words & Music by Noel Gallagher

C#m7
A maj9
blame it on___ the chang - in' of___ the sea - sons,___ the thoughts that I___ con - veyed.___
C#m7
A maj9
C#m7
A maj9
B
B/A
Does it make it al - right?
B/G#
B/F#
B
B/A
B/G#
B/F#
It does - n't make it al - right.___

E
F#7/E
A/E
To roll it ov - er my soul, leave me here.
E
F#7/E
Roll it ov - er my soul, leave me here.
A
G6
F#m7
1.
E
2.
E
Em7

A/E
E
Guitar
Em7
A/E
E
Em7
A/E
C/E
D/E
E
3

E
F#7/E
To roll it ov - er my soul, leave me here.
A/E
E
Roll it ov - er my soul,
F#7/E
1.
A/E
E
leave me here.
8vb
(8vb)

Verse 2:
Look around at all the plastic people
That live without a care
Try to sit with me around my table
But never bring a chair.

Does it make it alright?
It doesn't make it alright.

To roll it over *etc.*

Exclusive distributors:
Music Sales Limited
8/9 Frith Street, London W1V 5TZ, England.
Music Sales Pty Limited
120 Rothschild Avenue, Rosebery, NSW 2018, Australia.

Order No. AM964073
ISBN 0-7119-8178-7
This book © Copyright 2000 by Sony Music Publishing.

Unauthorised reproduction of any part of this
publication by any means including photocopying
is an infringement of copyright.

Music arranged by Derek Jones.
Music engraved by Paul Ewers Music Design.

Printed in the United Kingdom by
Caligraving Limited, Thetford, Norfolk.

Your Guarantee of Quality:
As publishers, we strive to produce every book to
the highest commercial standards.
The music has been freshly engraved and,
whilst endeavouring to retain the original running order
of the recorded album, the book has been carefully
designed to minimise awkward page turns and
to make playing from it a real pleasure.
Particular care has been given to specifying
acid-free, neutral-sized paper made from pulps which
have not been elemental chlorine bleached.
This pulp is from farmed sustainable forests and
was produced with special regard for the environment.
Throughout, the printing and binding have been
planned to ensure a sturdy, attractive publication
which should give years of enjoyment.
If your copy fails to meet our high standards,
please inform us and we will gladly replace it.

Music Sales' complete catalogue describes
thousands of titles and is available in full colour
sections by subject, direct from Music Sales Limited.
Please state your areas of interest and send
a cheque/postal order for £1.50 for postage to:
Music Sales Limited, Newmarket Road,
Bury St. Edmunds, Suffolk IP33 3YB.

www.musicsales.com